Ocean Grove Homes

A Walk Through Time

Erna M. Vanderberg

America Through Time®
Adding Color to American History

America Through Time is an imprint of Fonthill Media LLC
www.through-time.com
office@through-time.com

Published by Arcadia Publishing by arrangement with Fonthill Media LLC
For all general information, please contact Arcadia Publishing:
Telephone: 843-853-2070
Fax: 843-853-0044
E-mail: sales@arcadiapublishing.com
For customer service and orders:
Toll-Free 1-888-313-2665

www.arcadiapublishing.com

First published 2022

ISBN 978-1-63499-422-4

Typeset in Mrs Eaves XL Serif Narrow
Printed and bound in England

Introduction

Ocean Grove, known as "God's square mile at the Jersey Shore," has visitors in awe of an extensive collection of preserved Victorian-era homes. Among the eclectic assortment of homes, you will find a variety of shapes and sizes as well as the old along with the new. Any attempt to classify the older homes found in Ocean Grove has been difficult because original wood exterior ornamentation deteriorates over time. This book and walking tour attempts to capture an authentic collection of homes with characteristic elements to point us towards the original architectural heritage of Ocean Grove.

Published house design engravings in the 1880s as well as expanding railroad systems and modern manufacturing allowed for more diversity in Victorian architecture. The Ocean Grove Historic District Architectural Design Standards continue to preserve and maintain the town's architectural heritage. Some of the earliest key structures of the 1870s resembles the Stick style with decorated gable roof overhang and diagonal bracing. Later, more complex homes of the 1880s lean towards the Queen Anne style with irregular rooflines, asymmetrical façades, and machine-turned porch supports. Some historic homes mix and borrow from various architectural styles, sometimes labeled as Eclectic, Gothic, and Italianate with credit given to local artisans. Included are later structures like the sensible American Four Square and the artful Craftsman style, some of which were mail order kit homes.

The homes have been plotted onto a Google map for a self-guided walking tour.

Enjoy your walk through Ocean Grove Homes.

The past twenty-five years of my fifty-year architectural career has focused on the preservation, restoration, and design guidance of over 200 homes in the National Historic District of Ocean Grove, New Jersey. Magnificent open-air porches, period-style landscaped gardens, and elaborately tooled and handcrafted details by the many dedicated and uncelebrated artisans, have inspired those who have continued to steward the architectural treasures of this seaside square mile. The "Art of Historic Preservation" is best served when the past is both understood and respected. A *Walk Through Time* inspires us to do both.

Mark A. Pavliv, AIA/CID/NCARB

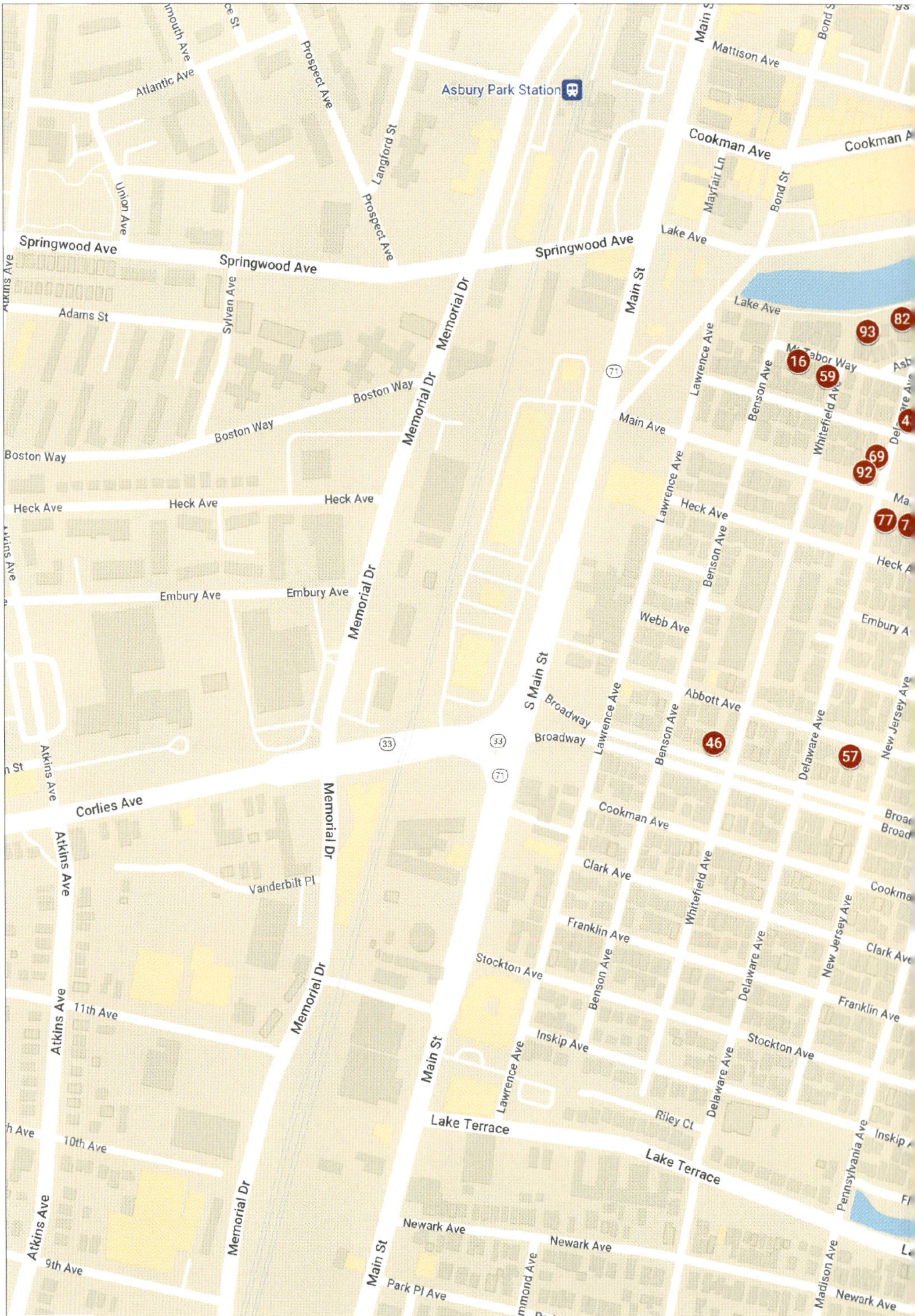
Asbury Park Station
Atlantic Ave
Prospect Ave
Langford St
Union Ave
Mattison Ave
Cookman Ave
Mayfair Ln
Bond St
Lake Ave
Springwood Ave
Springwood Ave
Springwood Ave
Main St
Adams St
Sylvan Ave
Memorial Dr
Lawrence Ave
Benson Ave
Whitefield Ave
Boston Way
Boston Way
Boston Way
Main Ave
Heck Ave
Heck Ave
Heck Ave
Heck Ave
Embury Ave
Embury Ave
Webb Ave
S Main St
Broadway
Broadway
Abbott Ave
Delaware Ave
Atkins Ave
Corlies Ave
Cookman Ave
Clark Ave
Vanderbilt Pl
Franklin Ave
New Jersey Ave
Stockton Ave
11th Ave
Inskip Ave
Stockton Ave
Riley Ct
Lake Terrace
Lake Terrace
10th Ave
Pennsylvania Ave
Newark Ave
Newark Ave
Newark Ave
9th Ave
Hammond Ave
Madison Ave
Park Pl Ave
Park Pl Ave
50m
16
46
57
59
69
77
82
92
93

Wesley Lake
Fletcher Lake
Lake Ave
Bangs Ave
Cookman Ave
Grand Ave
Spray Ave
Beach Ave
Boardwalk
Atlantic Ave
Kingsley Pl
Surf Ave
Asbury Ave
York Ave
Central Ave
Bath Ave
Pilgrim Pathway
Mt Carmel Way
Ocean Pathway
N Ocean Ave
McClintock St
Mt Hermon Way
Pitman Ave
Olin St
Pennsylvania Ave
Heck Ave
Main Ave
Embury Ave
New York Ave
Webb Ave
Abbott Ave
Broadway
Clark Ave
Franklin Ave
Lake Terrace
Kent Ave
Cliff Ave
Map data © 2022 Google

Ocean Grove's Victorian-era homes were constructed during the late 1800s when pattern designs became available, materials could be shipped via the railroads, and modernized machinery allowed for the manufacturing of complex shapes and elaborate decoration. Homes in the Grove tend to overlap, mix, and borrow from preceding architectural styles.

STICK STYLE can have a decorated front facing gable with overhanging eaves and stickwork with horizontal and vertical bands of texture and color.

EASTLAKE has rounder or turned forms and furniture like decorative accents.

ECLECTIC is a two-story home that varies individually with some decorative trim and round porch posts or columns.

FOLK VICTORIAN can have some decorative details on a simple shape. Decoration can be inspired by other styles with spindle work and a simple roof pediment.

QUEEN ANNE can have irregular shaped roof lines, asymmetrical porches along the front and vertical walls with patterns and decoration and a large chimney. Other identifiable elements can be Gothic, Italianate, French, or of Colonial Revival influences.

10 OCEAN AVE., *c.* 2015: This corner home, once the site of the old Queen Hotel, combines many Victorian design elements. The first two beach blocks have a flared setback to provide an unobstructed ocean view.

92 Heck Ave., *c.* 1905: Ocean Grove has other "Modern" homes built in the early 1900s. The Four Square is a two-story cube-shaped home with a pyramid roof and hipped roof dormers with classical porch columns. Some of these modern homes were mail order pre-cut pattern kits.

77 Stockton Ave., *c.* 1906: The Craftsman is a single-story home with low pitched gable roof, covered porch, exposed rafters, sometimes roof brackets, and tapered or square porch posts on piers.

SUMMER TENT HOMES: Summer tents have been an Ocean Grove tradition since 1870. Today, about 100 tents remain, compared to about 700 at one time. This generational ritual has created a perennial close-knit community. The front portion of the tent is positioned on a wooden platform with a canvas outer "fly," which protects from rain and sun. In the rear is a permanent wooden structure for cooking, toilet, shower, and winter storage.

The Great Auditorium of 1894: This Queen Anne and Stick-style structure remains the center of Ocean Grove religious and spiritual life. The irregular façade and front main gable have Gothic-style arches, three turrets, and metal ornamental wreaths. Ocean Grove grew rapidly as a Christian seaside community. This enormous structure was quickly completed with an almost 9,600-seat capacity for the 25th Camp Meeting anniversary.

BUNGALOW ON 64 CLARK AVE., *c.* 1880: This home was once a summer tent home, and by 1905, it became a permanent single-story dwelling. The canvas like roofline is decorated with wooden cutwork, reminiscent of a tent opening. The square porch posts are true early stick style and scroll saw cutouts may be local artisan design. The diamond shaped gable window provides light into the one-story space. This tiny cottage with small porch fits nicely on a narrow 30 × 60-foot Ocean Grove lot.

Cottage on 29 Bath Ave., *c.* 1870: This campground cottage is one of the earliest in Ocean Grove. The double doors are like a tent center opening and the home is about the same size as a summer tent. The wooden shutters with rounded tops and cut-out railings pay tribute to local artisans. The square porch posts with curved porch brackets preceded the mechanized lathe which allowed the rapid production of turned posts and other round forms found on later homes.

GOTHIC COTTAGE AT 76 MT. TABOR WAY, *c*. 1875: This small cross-gable two-story cottage has simple vertical board and batten siding and some flat cutout decoration. The porch posts are decorative and round, and the porch brackets are gently curved. The running trim along the roof line resembles lace, and the tiny decorative veranda makes it look like a miniature gingerbread house. The 1890 Sanborn map shows a two-story L-shaped dwelling with porch along the front.

GAMBREL COTTAGE AT 86 MT. TABOR WAY, *C.* 1880: This little cross gable home with first-floor porch looks like a bonnet trimmed with lace sometimes called a Dutch gambrel roof. The porch posts are turned and decorative with exposed rafter tails. The railing has vertical and horizontal lines to create squares and rectangles. A historic photo shows that Dr. Ward had a similar cottage on Ocean Ave. in 1875. (*Historical Society of Ocean Grove*)

Pioneer Cottage at 64 Asbury Ave., *c.* 1875: This home was one of the town's earliest cottages on the north end of town overlooking the lake. The wrapped porch with flat cutouts, round posts, and steep end gable can be considered an early Folk Victorian. The shed dormer and rear areas appear to have been added. The siding is wood shingles, and the use of color accentuates the variety of shapes and windows.

Stick at 5 Embury Ave., *c.* 1881: This appears to be a seaside cottage design from W. T. Comstock stone engravings with original board and batten siding, square sticks, and a gull-wing roofline. The front has floor to ceiling windows and shutters for fresh air. The upper porch gable is decorated with triangular scroll cutouts with an elegant center sash or tassel detail. The porch brackets are flat with scrolls and the posts are true square cut, Stick style.

Stick at 134 Mt. Tabor Way, c. 1870: This home was meticulously restored by the owner using an original stereoscopic image by G. W. Pach of N.Y. The winged canopy roofline has original exposed wooden roof rafters; it gracefully covers the second story porch. The porch posts and brackets are sticks and the railing and gable peak are simply adorned with diagonal sticks that form triangles like those found in pictures of the late Osborne Hotel.

STICK AT 8 HECK AVE., *c.* 1880: This simply and elegant Stick-style home has been in the Arnold family since 1906. The upper porch posts are still square sticks while a left-winged tent like canopy provides a graceful covering above the second-floor porch. The roof rafters are gently curved and exposed on the upper porch wing and overhang. The upper full-length windows, now door openings, are capped with a decorative cross board.

Stick at 13 Main Ave., *c.* 1875: This summer home has vertical wood siding and porch posts that are square sticks. The railing balusters are flat with cutouts giving the home a Swiss chalet feel. The scroll saw cutouts or fretwork and center arch breaks the overhang up into decorative sections that cast a patterned shadow. This home can be found in early Main Ave. postcards.

STICK AT 16 HECK AVE., *c.* 1870: This home shows off local artisan craftsmanship with scroll saw cutouts that resemble lace curtains. The porch posts are sticks and the porch brackets and roof brackets are fanciful scrolls of flat sawn wood. Full-length windows and doors with shutters allow for plenty of summer breezes. The two awning windows have stained glass decoration and the openings are topped with triangular pediments. The roofline has a graceful wing that works like a canopy.

Stick at 43 McClintock St., *c.* 1880: This historic museum house is maintained by the Historical Society of Ocean Grove. The rectangular box like home has true square stick porch posts and flat scrollwork as gable overhang decoration. The home has functional wood shutter for light control and airflow, while your horse hitch and steppingstone are conveniently located along the front.

STICK DUPLEX AT 35 OLIN ST., *c.* 1876: This duplex home has been preserved with original vertical siding, wooden windows, and an elaborate upper porch gable decoration. The overhang is decorated with an arch and the triangular sections create an interesting shade pattern of sticks and scrolls. The porch posts remain to be true thin sticks designed to hold up the upper porch and roof overhang. The upper spindles are decorative cut-outs.

Stick at 67 Webb Ave., *c.* 1876: This small-scale stick home has a decorated front facing gable and overhang with scroll saw cutouts and toothed edges. The porch balusters are flat cutouts, and the porch posts are true sticks with scrolled brackets. The center entry is double leafed, and the upper double doors are triangle-shaped, also found on 9 Pilgrim Pathway.

STICK AT 33 EMBURY AVE., *c.* 1877: This small-scale stick home with decorated gable overhang has operable wooden shutter and double-leafed doors and an upper rounded window. The porch posts are true small-scale square sticks, and three sections of the gable are decorated with arches and cutouts. The windows and doors have operable shutters for privacy and ventilation.

STICK AT 58 ASBURY AVE., *c.* 1875: This small-scale historic home has stick porch posts and simple diagonal and arched stick decoration. The tiny middle pent roof provides shade and rain covering for the lower porch and the upper porch overhang has simple timber like members. The round top windows and doors remain as well as an adjacent tent platform tiny home on the side.

Stick at 14 New York Ave., *c.* 1880: This stick home with wing has been rebuilt while the upper porch section remains stick with original rounded wooden windows with 4. The double leaf original front door is shown here. Later expansions are evident on the back of the home. The gentle canopy wing swoop may have been lost over the years and the lower porch posts are now turned.

STICK AT 47 WEBB AVE., *c.* 1883: This restored home has a main gable with an overhang and double porches supported by stick posts with curved flat brackets. The gable overhang is decorated with elaborate floral cutouts inside a triangular frame with center sash. The porch railing balusters are flat sawn cutouts while the windows and doors have a wide decorative surround and a peaked cross board.

Stick at 11 Ocean Pathway, c. 1876: This award-winning restored home has a wood shingle pattern on the pent porch roof as well as many other exquisite decorative details. The area below the gable includes a tiny open-air balcony with a wishbone arch and scroll saw cutouts. The risers on the steps have a diamond detail as well as the second-floor porch planters. Earliest photos do not show an upper balcony or pent roof on the first floor.

Eastlake at 3 Main Ave., *c.* 1876: This home is a typical two-story Eastlake Stick-style with porches, turned posts, and cutouts. The porch has curved brackets and round medallions. These porch posts and brackets can still be seen on a handful of porches around town along with the shoestring detail. The small round upper gable window remains for light as well as the stepped triple cross board detail, which can also be found on the upper front of pin 70.

Eastlake at 101 Mt. Tabor Way, c. 1880: This two-story duplex home has some of the best-preserved colored glass windows and double doors and gable decorations. Notice the double leafed center doors on both and the colored glass pieces in the entry doors. The gable peaks have been decorated with sticks and lace-like cutouts and the porch posts are thin turned posts with original flat leaf balusters also found on the back porch of pin 50 in this book.

Eastlake at 9 Ocean Pathway, *c.* 1876: This historic home has an enormous amount of ornamentation while an older photo show stick porch posts. This winged stick design has rounded porch posts and lots of scroll saw cutouts on the gable. The bottom railing has spool-shaped balusters and cutouts. The triangular entry has a carved decoration called an Eastlake decoration. The balcony was probably added when the posts were changed.

EASTLAKE AT 7 OCEAN PATHWAY, *C.* 1876: This preserved Stick-style home has lots of street-side Eastlake decoration that honors local artisan craftsmanship. The windows and doors are outlined, and the porch posts and brackets are decorative. The upper porch has a gull wing. The openings are outlined with a patterned surround and capped with peaks and decorations. Sticks were probably changed to rounded posts and the balcony was added.

Eastlake at 4½ Atlantic Ave., c. 1885: This double porch and Stick-style gable is decorated with turned posts and many triangular cutouts. The balusters are a repeating pattern of flat cutouts. The gable is divided into three sections with triangular cutwork and an arched center section. Victorian paint colors have a subdued earthy palette, and here there are four colors of paint. Similar to 8 Olin St., decoration is limited to the front.

EASTLAKE AT 6 ATLANTIC AVE. AND SURF AVE., *c.* 1884: This amazing former grand hotel has been converted into two/two family homes (four lots) by addition of a center firewall. Old photographs were used for the restoration and original columns were duplicated at great expense. The complicated roofline includes a gullwing and dormers. The gables and porch brackets and railings are decorated with open lace like cutwork in weather-resistant materials.

Eclectic Victorian at 99 Mt. Hermon Way, *c.* 1870: This eclectic Victorian home has wood lap siding, turned porch posts and an original round attic window with wooden shutters. The gable is outlined in scalloped running trim along with a triangular cutout decoration and roof scroll at the peak. This is an example of front decoration on a simple rectangular house on a narrow and long 30 × 60-foot lot.

Eclectic Victorian at 7 Olin St., *c.* 1873: This is an early small-scale two-story home with rounded double leaf doors and arched top windows upper sticks and lower round columns. The upper porch posts are square cut sticks, and the canopy is divided into three sections with open cutouts that resemble lace. Notice the little round window and the very low upper porch railing. This street does not have a flared setback.

Eclectic Victorian at 17 Surf Ave., *c.* 1870: This corner home has been preserved through time to showcase Ocean Grove's earliest artisans. The showy front gable with flared winged canopy has stick upper porch posts and arched braces and cutouts and medallions. The side bay has octagon shingles and panels and an upper round top wooden window. The window and door casings and top decorations are decorative while the bottom porch posts are now round.

ECLECTIC VICTORIAN AT 15 OCEAN PATHWAY, *c.* 1890: This corner stick cross gable has been completely restored with gingerbread decoration and flat sawn porch balusters. The front gable overhang covers the second-story porch and the upper balcony. The front has centered double doors and the side has an irregular roof line, a decorated two-story bay and gothic-peaked window, and a dormer on the third floor.

Eclectic Victorian at 9 Pilgrim Pathway, *c.* 1875: This cottage may have had stick porch posts which were later replaced with round posts. The upper double leaf door is triangular at the top as well as the matching louver door. The short "pent" roof provides shade and rain protection on the lower porch much like an awning would. The double leaf door detail can also be seen on pin 22 in this book. The upper spindle design was suggested by T. Bell.

Eclectic Victorian at 58 Lake Ave., *c.* 1890: This restored eclectic home sits proudly overlooking the lake. The owner tells me that Dr. Cookman a generous man lived here and that the Ocean Grove founders probably pitched their tents on the lawn overlooking Wesley Lake. The many Queen Anne features include a turret and colored glass windows as well as a side gable pediment tree detail along with the scalloped siding.

ECLECTIC VICTORIAN AT 19 ABBOTT AVE., *C.* 1890: This home with a clipped-end gable has a side flare detail. The irregular roof line has triangular clipped peaks and a dormer as well as a side veranda. The porch entry pediment is a sunburst. The porch is covered, and the posts are turned. The upper siding is scalloped and there is a triangular window detail. Homes in the first two beach blocks enjoy a flared setback.

Eclectic Victorian at 31 Pitman Ave., *c.* 1890: This home combines a few Ocean Grove design elements and styles. The front gable has a Stick-style double porch without roof overhang. The porch posts are turned, and the railing is an open geometric or Chippendale design. The third floor has a balcony with gable peak pediment with ball drop and finial pinnacle.

Eclectic Victorian at 74 Mt. Tabor Way, *c.* 1880: This home has well-preserved gable decoration above the second-floor porch and original wood lap siding. The porch posts are round, and the porch brackets are curved cutouts with lots of round rosette decorations. The side has a projecting bay with decorative panels and brackets. The owner tells me the home had many little rooms with individual sinks.

Eclectic Victorian at 113 Mt. Hermon Way, *c.* 1880: Here you see a winged cross-gable corner home with two porches that allow for plenty of fresh air and shade. The bay windows on the side gable provide a variety of shapes. The porch posts appear to have been boxed in and the porch brackets are curved with a center detail. The local Rev. Beegle of Camp Meeting lived here in a smaller, simpler corner cross gable.

ECLECTIC VICTORIAN AT 68 LAKE AVE., *c.* 1885: This was the original location of the home of Dr. Ellwood Stokes, the Ocean Grove visionary. The square tower has a low-profile hipped roof, and the veranda is quite broad. The siding is broad boards with a triplet and the roof line is varied with a center gable and bay as well as a hexagonal tower on the side with an enclosed porch. In the background is the Great Auditorium (pin 9).

Eclectic Victorian at 26 Lake Ave., *c.* 1890: This award-winning home has been completely restored and expanded. Hidden inside is an original foursquare with hipped roof while the Queen Anne porch tower is prominent with raised panel porch column details and dentil trim. Look for a sunroom and balcony and stained-glass windows within a very protective hedge as well as premium, flawless wood materials on the exterior.

FOLK VICTORIAN AT 129 BROADWAY, *c.* 1880: The owner of this home tells me that the balloon framing had to be modified for improved fire safety before move-in by adding fire stops between floors. The decorative porch has original sunbursts and upper spools as well as round porch posts with sunburst details. The remainder of the gable is simple with exposed rafters and ball drops and a peaked pinnacle.

FOLK VICTORIAN AT 80 MT. ZION WAY, *C.* 1885: This main gable corner home with asymmetrical original porch is called the Dutch Farmhouse. The showcase original porch is painted primarily in historic Van Deusen blue. Another original part of this home are the double leafed doors and the original "Ring" doorbell. Notice the original round exposed porch rafter tails and upper spool-shaped spindles.

FOLK VICTORIAN 84 MT. CARMEL WAY, *c.* 1880: This two-story home is narrow, tall, and long with street-side decoration and a side bay. The front peaked window toppers appear to be held up with decorative brackets. The owners love their summer house and side yard along with what probably was a tent and now converted into a small cottage great for kids and guests.

Folk Victorian at 23 Webb Ave., *c.* 1881: This cottage home is a gem waiting to be restored. Underneath the siding there may be more original details to be discovered. This seaside cottage design has an L-shaped floor plan with two porches. The Gothic-like gable canopy with scroll saw cutwork may be credited to local artisans like pin 36 in this book.

Folk Victorian at 89 Mt. Hermon Way, *c.* 1880: This corner home has square upper porch posts and updated classic posts on the lower porch. The gable is broken up into three decorated sections that include arches and triangles with cutouts. The owner used dental tools to uncover the original porch balusters on the side porch. Look at those amazing original decorative brackets and decorative panels along the side bay.

Folk Victorian at 37 Atlantic Ave., *c.* 1878: This corner cross gable has a second-story porch overhang that has been decorated with local artisan cutouts. The upper square sticks hold up the decorative gable overhang while the lower porch has classical columns and a short pent roof overhang. Victorian-era railings were quite low, and additional lattice has been added to the upper porch railing for safety.

GOTHIC COTTAGE AT 62 HECK AVE., *c.* 1890: This home has a steep gable and a broad decorated trim board or bargeboard with finial drops and a finial pinnacle. The lower entry doors are round double leafed and the front windows are round top. The home sits on a corner with a cross gable. The porch railings are decorative openwork, and the upper siding is a scalloped pattern above horizontal siding.

GOTHIC COTTAGE AT 22 SURF AVE., *c.* 1885: This home has a decorated front gable and balcony with Chippendale-style railings. The porch posts are turned, and the lower siding is horizontal while the upper siding is vertical. The windows are round top and surrounded by trim. The main roof gable is decorated with posts, finials, and decorative bargeboard pieces.

ITALIANATE AT 91 ASBURY AVE., *C.* 1876: This century home has original scalloped siding and cornice details with brackets. The center appears to be a small Italian-influenced square tower, the porch columns are classical, and the bay windows are projecting and bracketed on both cross gables. The attic windows are gothic with a steep roofline and brackets and cornice detail.

ITALIANATE AT 37 OCEAN PATHWAY, *c.* 1875: This corner duplex home was once a more elaborate Second Empire Victorian with cupola and now has a mansard roof. The underside roof cornice has double brackets and the middle windows have elaborate arches while the dormers have a peak. The red-patterned mansard roof angle is straight, and the entry has two sets of double-leafed doors.

Second Empire at 92 Lake Ave., *c.* 1890: This home overlooking Wesley Lake borrows from the French with a flared mansard roof, a corniced square tower with brackets, and round top roof windows. The lakeside asymmetrical porch has classic tapered columns, straight balusters, and a double leafed glass entry.

Second Empire at 106 Abbott Ave., *c.* 1904: This tiny award-winning two-story home is only 850 sq. ft. The mansard roof provides more room on the second floor. The shutters are wood, and the wood lap siding runs along the sides. This tent-sized house with a tiny porch is nestled between a row of Ocean Grove Homes and some trees.

QUEEN ANNE AT 92 MT. CARMEL WAY, *c.* 1876: This century home uses a Victorian color scheme to highlight the side gable and bay windows. The decorative railing and finials are nicely preserved as well as the shutters and lap siding. The gable pediments, scroll saw cut work, stick drops, and porch railing have been preserved with many layers of paint.

QUEEN ANNE AT 128 MT. TABOR WAY, *c.* 1880: This refurbished corner cross gable has Queen Anne-style windows, exposed rafters, and a double leaf front entry. The siding is broken up with horizontal and vertical lines and each gable is adorned with scalloped siding and side cornice. The bargeboard or fascia have medallions and grooves.

Queen Anne at 5 Ocean Pathway, *c.* 1879: Four former presidents had dinner at this home, including Roosevelt, who gave a speech from the balcony. The home was probably renovated around the turn of the century and once connected to the twin next door. The stained-glass transoms are elaborate and similar on both homes.

Queen Anne at 13 Ocean Pathway, *c.* 1876: This home has some arched window mullions and a hexagonal tower. The main roof gable is steep and outlined with cornice and decorated with patterned shingles along with a window sunburst, cross board, and bracket. The columns and the porch balusters were probably part of a classical renovation.

Queen Anne at 90 Webb Ave., *c.* 1890: This corner cross-gable home has a square tower, wood siding and shutters and a large porch. The porch posts are turned with curved porch brackets, and upper spindles are also found on pins 46 and 47 in this book. The top has scalloped siding, the tower has brackets while the gable eaves are trimmed with a toothed edge and cutouts, and I see a colorful glass window.

Queen Anne at 91 Mt. Hermon Way, *c.* 1885: This corner gable home known as the Chadwick Cottage has colorful Queen Anne windows throughout, a dominant front decorated gable, and an asymmetrical porch. The shutters and siding are wood while the side bay and upper gable has scalloped shingles and a diamond pattern. The porch columns appear to be boxed in.

QUEEN ANNE AT 74 MAIN AVE., *C.* 1876: This corner home has a decorated front gable with a cross gable. The gable overhang has a flared kick and brackets. The bay windows and triple windows have arched decorative mullions. The porch has an upper beading detail while the gable peak also has a decorated overhang with projecting rafter tails.

QUEEN ANNE AT 44 CENTRAL AVE., *c.* 1904: This front gable home is elaborate with a gambrel cross gable and overhang, garland decoration, brackets, and flared detail. The asymmetrical porch has a decorative triangular side entry. The brick chimney is grand as well as the contrasting patterned roof and wooden clipped shingles and numerous brackets that appear under the overhang.

QUEEN ANNE AT 44 WEBB AVE., *c.* 1890: This grand home has a slate and patterned roof. The lap siding is heavily decorated below the roofline with patterned shingles. The tallest tower is impressive with multiple rows of color and texture and rosettes. The original Queen Anne windows remain with decorative casing and triangular peaked pediments.

QUEEN ANNE AT 7 EMBURY AVE., *c.* 1890: This three-story home has many colorful Queen Anne windows. The center entry has a bay tower on the right and smaller gable on the left. The siding is scalloped, and the porch posts are round, the brackets curved with an upper open detail. The gable peak has a colorful half-round window and round fascia decoration.

Queen Anne at 73 Main Ave., c. 1890: This home provides plenty of original decorative architectural detail. The asymmetrical façade has an end tower, center portico, and towering chimney. The railings and upper porch spindles have seen many layers of paint. The roof underside edge is decorated, and the dormers are angled with curved peaks.

QUEEN ANNE AT 115 MAIN AVE., *c.* 1890: This cross-gable home was once the home of Dr. Alday, a physician, minister, and Camp Meeting trustee. The owners have since uncovered the original details. The gables have diagonal siding, a cornice detail, and sunbursts. The front window and door have an amazing transom of colored glass.

Queen Anne at 90 Mt. Tabor Way, *c.* 1890: This cross-gable home has many colorful windows and a tower added around 1905. The horizontal wood siding is broken up with scalloped shingles and decorative corner cornice. The tower has a kicked-out flare and decorative detail below the roofline. The columns appear to be boxed in and classical on the upper porch.

Queen Anne at 107 Central Ave., *c*. 1890: This renovated home has an enormous curved asymmetrical porch for taking in views. The windows, diamond siding, turret, irregular roofline, and asymmetrical façade is all part of the Queen Anne style. The owners wonder if the original smaller main house could have been moved across Fletcher Lake on ice.

QUEEN ANNE VICTORIAN AT 18 SEAVIEW AVE., *c.* 1890: This corner home has a round tower, extensive wrapped, curved porch, an irregular roofline, hooded dormers with timberline decoration, turned porch posts, and graciously curved porch brackets as well as numerous colored glass windows. The cross-gable fascia boards are a grooved pattern. The home is the mirror image of pin 73.

QUEEN ANNE VICTORIAN AT 17 ABBOTT AVE., *c.* 1890: The owners of this elaborate home uncovered and renovated this corner gem. A New York socialite once used the home for entertaining the likes of Helen Hayes. The current owner wonders if a mirror image of this home exists on the other side of town because a former owner had two daughters. See pin 72.

QUEEN ANNE VICTORIAN AT 62 WEBB AVE., *c.* 1890: This restored corner Queen Anne is the joy and pride of the current owners who have done most of the work themselves. The center tower has upper half windows with medallions and texture. The corner porch provides for plenty of visiting with friends and neighbors and the back area is great for grilling.

Queen Anne Victorian at 15 Ocean Ave., *c.* 1890: This corner Queen Anne home has a curved wrap porch and most likely great ocean views. The tower with dentil trim has original windows with curved original glass. The triangular porticos have inset sunburst details. The small back porch has original tuned porch posts found on other homes in the grove.

QUEEN ANNE VICTORIAN AT 89 MT. CARMEL WAY, *C.* 1890: This corner cross-gable home once was the meeting place for the local women's club. There also was a time when it served as the local library with a small theater. Notice the upper cross-gable cornice returns and the wrapping porch, center tower, and the triple window sunburst details. The siding may be covering some other hidden decorative details.

QUEEN ANNE VICTORIAN AT 112 MAIN AVE., *C.* 1890: This renovated cross gable with trapezoid inner roof and corner tower is complete with gas lanterns. The front wrapping porch brackets have delicate decorative details, and the tower is decorated with scalloped siding and rosettes. The simple gable fascia board design borrows from the past with some grooves and a sawtooth edge, while the gable peaks have a stick pediment and drop.

QUEEN ANNE AT 108 MAIN AVE., *C.* 1890: This home has lots of decoration and an interesting irregular roofline complete with dormers and a round tower. Look for original windows on the second floor and the sunburst details on the porch brackets. The porch posts are turned, and the railing has an open design. The wrought iron fence surrounds the yard.

Queen Anne at 92 Mt. Zion Way, c. 1904: This home with Beaux Arts decorations is quite elaborate. The front façade has a decorated gable, cornices, swags, dentil trim, and faux joist ends. The tower bottom is split face block at the base with patterned shingles. The tower windows have original round glass. A charitable female doctor once owned the home and left her apothecary cabinet.

QUEEN ANNE AT 43 ABBOTT AVE., *c.* 1881: This home called Rainbow Cottage has a unique irregular roofline that consists of a trapezoid roof with large and small triangular gables. The asymmetrical porch has upper spindles, turned posts, and decorative brackets. The windows have multiple square panes, and the upper corners are decorated.

Queen Anne at 19 Ocean Pathway, *c.* 1890: This Queen Anne-style cross gable home is now a guesthouse with plenty of decorative details. The gable fascia has a shoestring design, and the peaks are decorated with sticks and brackets. The original entry was along the side with a porch. The home was updated with classical columns and patterned roof shingles.

Winged Cross Gable at 118 Lake Ave., *c.* 1890: This may be the only remaining example of a winged cross-gable home. Some original elements suggest stick gable decoration while the two-story bay has a cornice and brackets like pin 50. The upper porch columns appear to be camphor sticks while redundant railing suggest additional changes.

Seaside Colonial Eclectic at 49 Abbott Ave., *c.* 1906: Parts of this design appear in the Comstock architectural engravings of colonial cottages. The home was once owned by the famous Tali Essen Morgan, the Camp Meeting musical director of choir festivals, pageants, and youth programs. The musical home has also heard the singing of Enrico Caruso, the Italian opera singer.

CLIPPED CROSS GABLE AT 93 CENTRAL AVE., *c.* 1885: This corner cross-gable roofline reminds me of a farmhouse in Holland. The bonnet-style gambrel roof has gable truss work or stick-like members. A flower-shaped window is tucked underneath the roof canopy. The porch posts resemble sticks while the dormer gives extra space and light.

CLIPPED CROSS GABLE AT 79 BROADWAY, *C.* 1885: This corner cross gable has clipped ends or gambrel ends and many original colorful Queen Anne windows. The third floor has been expanded with a dormer in the roofline. The owner thinks the small hexagon peak was relocated to the back. The gables have original patterned shingles and color. Look for wavy original glass windows.

CLIPPED CROSS GABLE AT 9 OCEAN AVE., *c.* 1890: This home has an irregular roof line with an original L-shaped cross gable the has been clipped. The tower and dormer probably were added, and the second-floor wrap porch has been enclosed to gain living space. The round hoods at the top of the gable have a vine shaped pattern also found on pin 87.

Clipped Cross Gable at 62 Lake Ave., *c.* 1890: This cross-gable home overlooking Wesley Lake has a two-story porch and irregular roofline. The folded or clipped gable ends look like they have a bonnet. Earlier lake pictures show a one-story porch. The porch posts are turned and the vine like upper cutouts are like pin 86.

Colonial Revival at 5 Pitman Ave.: This home started out as a 1923 Sears & Roebuck modern home kit called the Lexington. The home was one of the highest priced kit models advertised as "already cut" and fitted for $4,472. The home was considered a nine-room colonial with traditional detailing and many windows—very comfortable in any location. The first- and second-floor porches and dormers have been upgraded.

COLONIAL REVIVAL AT 130 LAKE AVE., *c.* 1910: This simply grand two-story home with cornice overlooking Wesley Lake is called "Briarcliff." The long front edge has a porch with tapered classical columns and a grand chandelier. The tall windows and dormers with round top windows display simple elegance. The gable ends have lattice windows and an upper gothic window detail with cornice returns and brackets.

Four Square at 91 Mt. Carmel Way, *c.* 1925: This Mission-style Four Square has stucco siding commonly found on the Sears & Roebuck "Alhambra" home kit in 1923 for $2,998. The front has a double porch with restored decorative stone columns to match the large decorative stone side fireplace. The multiple windowpane squares are throughout.

Four Square at 91 Mt. Tabor Way, *c.* 1915: The owners of this home tell me that this comes from the Sears & Roebuck mail-order catalog. The hipped roof has hipped roof dormers. The side has a two-story angled bay with wave-like shingles, which could be a customization. The angled bays break up the cube like shape and horizontal lap siding.

CRAFTSMAN COTTAGE AT 117 MAIN AVE., *c.* 1910: This side gable home has tapered porch columns along with a matching tapered brick fireplace. The roof gable also has a flared kick, which serves as the awning for the covered porch. The second story has a dormer with paired windows. The upper siding is stained cedar, and the lower half is a horizontal pattern.

CRAFTSMAN COTTAGE AT 132 LAKE AVE., *c.* 1910: The side gable roof on this cottage has a dormer with 3 grouped double hung windows and exposed rafter tails. The porch posts suggest a vine trellis. Some of the siding is a brick like veneer. A mail order pre-cut home kit could be shipped by railroad for a great price.

Queen Anne at 75 Cookman Ave., *c.* 2018: This new construction Queen Anne has an asymmetrical façade, bracketed tower to the left of the front-facing gable with shingle and lap siding, and a porch with turned columns and straight spindles. The tower has rectangular panel decoration, a flared detail, and a variety of shapes and colors. This new home fits seamlessly into the neighborhood while the materials and design are smarter and earth friendly.

CRAFTSMAN AT 102 MT. TABOR AVE., *c.* 2018: This home is an example of a new construction stitched into the existing fabric of Ocean Grove homes. The tapered columns sit on a cedar shingle base and stone piers. The siding is fire retardant material. The dormer has a triplet of grouped windows. The roof is flared out to form the covered porch and the colors are natural while the gutter downspouts are whimsical rain chains.

Acknowledgments

Many thanks to the wonderful homeowners of Ocean Grove who love preserving a piece of American history.

Bell, Wayne T., and Christopher M. Flynn, *Ocean Grove in Vintage Postcards* (Arcadia, 2004)

Bell, Wayne T. *Ocean Grove. Images of America Ocean Grove* (Arcadia, 2000)

Boyd, Jennifer, G. Hunton. *A Home Renovator's Guide for Historic Ocean Grove* (1989)

Comstock, William T. *Victorian Domestic Architectural Plans and Details* (Dover Publications, 1987)

Fox, David H. *Fox's Directory of Ocean Grove* (Flushing, L.I., N.Y. 2020)

Hendrickson, Richard. *A Christian Walking Tour of Ocean Grove*

Historical Society of Ocean Grove, historicalsocietyofoceangrove.org

McAlester, Virginia, and A. Lee McAlester. *A Field Guide to American Houses: The Definitive Guide to Identifying and Understanding America's Domestic Architecture* (Alfred A. Knopf, 2019)

Ocean Grove Camp Meeting Association, oceangrove.org

Pavliv, Mark A. *Ocean Grove Historic District Architectural Design Guidelines for Residential Structures.* 2005.

"Sanborn." *Princeton University*, The Trustees of Princeton University, library.princeton.edu/libraries/firestone/rbsc/aids/sanborn/monmouth/ocean-grove.html.